# APOCRYPHAL GENESIS

## TRAVIS MOSSOTTI

 saturnalia | BOOKS

Distributed by Independent Publishers Group
Chicago

Saturnalia Books
2816 North Kent Rd.
Broomall, PA 19008
info@saturnaliabooks.com

ISBN: 978-1-947817-62-3 (print), 978-1-947817-63-0 (ebook)
Library of Congress Control Number: 2023943655

Cover art by Josh Mossotti
Book design by Robin Vuchnich

Distributed by:
Independent Publishing Group
814 N. Franklin St.
Chicago, IL 60610
800-888-4741

*For my mother and my father,*
*who set my boat into the water*
*and taught me to row*

It is like what we imagine knowledge to be:

dark, salt, clear, moving, utterly free,

drawn from the cold hard mouth

of the world, derived from the rocky breasts

forever, flowing and drawn, and since

our knowledge is historical, flowing, and flown.


—*Elizabeth Bishop, "At the Fishhouses"*

# WHEREFROM COMES THIS COUNTRY GOES

Comes our patron city of burnt-clay façades
                into the canonized American heart gone quaked
                                and split and sown. Goes the flame-raked
                smokestack estate plan drawn out one thousand
generations until our lovechild escapes to a river
                surrounded by dust that swishes its flit and grain
                                into the wind of grit and scour. Comes
                a yelpish bang ka-ching from faraway kingdoms
of registers rung to our wasteland landfills and roil.
                Goes the nerve-wracked birds to rally black batons.
                                Comes the blotter stains whorling and vanishing
                into scrimmages where bone breaks get set
back into place with mortar and red brick. Goes
                the healing into the moon-whelped spring singing
                                chrysalis, singing hoarfrost, singing gravestone.
                I call forth a bustle of veiled debutantes
kerchiefing tears from church bells which loll

in warped towers—I call and the fireclay comes.

        I call forth a gramophone sipping Stack-O-Lee

on a wraparound porch, some backwater asylum,

and the needle scrapes like a canoe run ashore.

        I call forth the flight feathers of crows and watch

                as they unstitch butternut from blackhaw,

        ash from sweetgum—I call and the brick kilns come.

I call forth the bellows and the fires stoked

        until they reach the sweet red color of hell,

                the fervor of flame snap and the seam peels away.

        I call forth the prefab floodplain churches

and the mob bosses teetering on the threshold

        of bootleg nirvana—I call and the warehouses come.

        I call and the whole goddamned country comes.

        I whistle and this city snaps its heels at attention.

I sing of this home I sing of thee and I sing America

        strung up by its ankles and slit from nape to nuts.

        I sing Mississippi and I sing of my palatial,

my watery commerce, blessed with wide hips

and easy birth. I sing wherefrom comes this country.

I sing and it goes back to the place where crowns

are restored to derecho-snapped old-growth oaks.

To where the Atlantic and Pacific lap their waves

against Ouachita mountain peaks and the sun

fiddles a final arrow loose from his quiver,

and the moon falls asleep atop her last

barrel of wine wherein ferments the original

darkness. That we may drink from it and be

healed, that we may drink from it and be broken.

יְשֵׁת

And whence they came and whither they shall go
The dew upon their feet shall manifest.

—*Wallace Stevens, "Sunday Morning"*

# APOCRYPHAL GENESIS

The banal loomed large. Windows fogged up
and emojis were fingered upon the glass panes.
Out of the wider bends of Mississippi river mud
crept the creepers that creepeth, while flames licked
clay to fashion bricks for the first Savings and Loan.
Orchid labella unfurled—someone leaned in and said,
*my, my, my,* while God kept laying two-dollar pony bets
and losing his shirt and wrinkling down the foreskin
of a paper sack and tilting his bottle filled with god
knows what. The sky not yet entirely aflame. Face
of the waters of corporate fountains still profitable,
and on the sixth day, a ragtag group of engineers
slipped on the condoms of creation and flagged
the first outpost on Mars as you overslept (king-sized)
and missed your own coronation. Waters did rise
and rise and the polar caps were like, *Whatever,*
which was the typical response from their generation.
*Whatever,* said the mountains laid plane, and,
*Whatever,* said the reefs melting like candle wax.
*Whatever,* said the carboniferous bones sludging
tarpit remains where once proud jungles stood
and brought forth friendlier cyclones. Raindrops

tapped against the stream of consciousness like a junkie
looking for his one good vein, waiting for the last
wild thing in Heaven to become undeniably reasonable.

# CONTEMPLATION OF A LIVE OAK IN SAN ANTONIO

If I contemplate this tree the wrong way,
I might conclude it's not a tree at all, which
may indicate that all beauty has evaporated
at last from the world leaving only what
shocks us awake at night, and what good
would that do anyone? No, I conclude this
crooked finger reaching from the earth
is, in fact, a tree—not a symbol or sign
of the density of solid matter. Not a theory
bending towards uniformity or grace under
the pressure of indifferent weather. Not
a new breed of cancer or the pummeling
of hammer on rock. Not bread or discourse
or atmospheric anomaly. I admire how
the skin of the tree stiffens to bark, gray
as a man's beard in the autumn of his life,
and its leaves rest still upon the still air.
One could paint this tree for hours on end
and the only noticeable change would be
angled light, hues, shadow filling the bark's
crevasses, darkness spilling over into deeper
shades of black and then the moon grinding

its teeth while dreams begin convalescing:
anger and faith and mild forms of retribution,
telescopes scraping deeper into the womb
of the universe in the way we've all become
accustomed to. By nature, I'm not an alarmist,
but I believe this single tree is a problem
we've yet to solve and it's so obviously here,
just an arm's length away, jutting up from soil
and compacted rock and breathing, yes
breathing, and speaking the language of time
so we might venture to touch it and feel
for once some peace we've forgotten
or given up on entirely. There it is though,
in the space between the whirl of electrons.

# BOOK(S) OF THE DEAD

*Don't shine what's expendable.*
—Charles Wright, "Lives of The Artists"

Beauty, beauty, beauty, beauty be damned.
K was not a poet of acclaim—a few journal
appearances, but he never published a book
of his own and died at 49 from cancer. I'm not
sure what any of this means. K was an adjunct
with no health insurance in these United States.
His death was likely preventable. This isn't
beautiful poetry because the story is ugly
and because mercy sure as hell isn't charity.
And so K died and the English Department
hosted a memorial service and gave away
his books because he had no family to take on
his library—a library isn't charity or mercy,
just words stacked vertically, pressed firmly
front to back. And so I took a few books, and inside
*Black Zodiac* by Charles Wright at the poem
"Lives of The Artists" I found a ticket stub
for a Yankees game from '96. Yankees won.
Three for fifteen with runners in scoring position
isn't the best, but they won the regular season

game, and K left the stub at this poem for me
to find. Wright says, the true word / Is the word
about the word, but K might have taken his father
to the game and perhaps didn't discuss poetry
or beauty or the word about the word about
the word. And because he flagged the poem
at the poem's first page, I can't say for certain
if he actually read the poem and meant to highlight
the poem, or if the poem is as far as he made it
into the book? Only K knows for sure. My muse
is pissed as hell I'm writing this poem—she likes
music and form and this ain't got none of that.
The glue grows brittle in the bindings. The pages
yellow and our eyes grow weak—even our own
understanding of the words fades to dribble.
K should've gotten a better shake, but it doesn't
mean we're all alone in our little poetry silo.
Wright says, learn how to model before you learn
to finish things. He was quoting Michelangelo.

# BEVERLY THOMAS

Whatever business brings folks like you here
isn't any of hers, because Beverly Thomas
didn't become the queen of local real estate
by making assumptions. She just wants
to drive you around town and show you
what's available and won't hesitate to put
a finger on your lips to stop you at the $v$
and say, honey, Bev's enough. You study
her like an archeological artifact. Her hair
rests coifed in the branded perfection
of a high-school yearbook photo that's
blossomed into billboard, ageless and digital,
as she curls her manicured fingers around
the steering wheel of her Range Rover
and drives you through a flat town that seems
lit from every angle. You're supposed
to notice how the moisturizers and creams
keep her neck and chest firm as trout lips
nipping lures, and if conversation dips
a bit between properties she'll point out
the local catfish joint—secret is the heat
of the oil, she might say, but her eyes

sink back a bit and grow restless as she
begins staring off into a bank of trees, mostly
young cedar and pin oak, the occasional
paw paw, and the ever-present alchemy
of rain and stone carving new caves below.
Bev knows you're not buying, but she didn't
get this far by letting people like you go
home empty handed. When you step
out of her vehicle for the last time, she
watches you with the guarded optimism
of a widower, waves goodbye as you drive away.
A town inside her getting smaller and smaller.

# MISSING THE FARM

Here's the orchard someone else will tend to.
And the crawl space beneath the porch
of the house where someone else's barn cat
will slumber through the summer nights
dreaming of long-tailed mice in the high grass.
Over that field, the light dips and refracts
through the broken glass of the muck pond
where a catfish will take someone else's bait
and hook—that it might meet the refined
heat of a skillet. The ghosts of a thousand
head of cattle walk through the woods at night
in someone else's dream while the windows,
cracked slightly, let a mild breeze pass
through the empty rooms like an appraiser.
There is no death that cannot be undone
by simply turning the compost with a pitchfork
or by scattering scratch in the dirt for chickens
who sing each time they lay, but every repair
is only a gesture against the torment of slow
winds and steady rain and heavy sun. It will be
someone else who grows too old to climb
the ladder into the barn's cool loft or the flight

of stairs that lead to and from their own bed.
It will be their hand weighing the mortgage.
It will be their face forgetting its smile. Listen,
if the well pump kicks to life at dawn, it will be
someone else drawing a bath for the last time—
joints relaxing as their form submerges, body
recovering and failing in the same held breath.

## DU JOUR

I'm awake again. What more do you want?
I'm too domesticated, too ritualized,
too gutted, too after-the-fact and homely.
I see the yawp of my open dishwasher and
think the greens blended into my morning
smoothie means I'm on some fad or cancer
diet—diet of the failing state that follows
home the failed statesman to his house
with its failing cinderblock foundation
that inspires the crescendo of his failing
marriage—no. That's wrong. It's too early
in this poem for abstraction or politics.
What trust have I built? Let's try this.
It seems obvious (to me at least) that one
can only have one love or two at most,
but neither of those should be one's own
house shoes because comfort is boredom
taking root. How deep does one delve
into a singular thought before the thought
dissolves like sugar into batter or bursts
into a supernova, which is enlightenment
I imagine, but this sentence is a question?
Where did I go wrong in life? Where did I

go right? You can't compromise without
promise, but what happens if you have
your fingers crossed behind your back
in the old schoolyard style? My generation
is the one that traded in the rocket pack of youth
for the hum of a leafblower in the distance
that seems to be blowing the same spot
between the hours of eight and nine AM
every morning. Am I the only one who looks
at their 401k and thinks it's time to retire
the idea of retirement? There's no green
pasture out there for poets like myself.
There's no anchor that can't be weighed
in the night whilst I sleep below deck.
I can swim, but I'm terrified of the water
and open water the most. I mean, I just
had to double check the definition of sextant
to be sure I used it right, and then I deleted
the line because I don't trust extended
metaphor. Who would? They're like lies
compounding interest when I don't have
enough for the monthly minimum due.

Falling asleep last night, my wife asked
why I haven't written about the protests,
fascists, environmental crisis, etc., and
I went on rubbing her back to get the knots
out then woke up to a cup of coffee,
let the chickens from the coop and sat
down on the porch to write this poem.
You tell me: what else should I have done?
What would you have done? What does
anger beget the alcoholic trying to stay
clean amidst a pandemic? I've learned
it may be best to simply try and understand
oneself before the end comes, to understand
the blue shell of a robin's egg in the yard
means both life and death, to understand
and listen to my neighbor when he leans
on the fence post to confess his daughter
was just diagnosed with throat cancer.
Sometimes, when I rub my wife's back,
as night drifts off into familiar black,
it's not enough to help her fall asleep.
She asks me to tell her a story and I try.

## UNIVERSAL

Woke up to the neighbor's great
Pyrenees pup bothering the run, flock
losing their minds and feathers
and trumpeting terrified alarms,
and when I yelled at the young dog
from the backdoor stoop, I did so in my
underwear, and the yearling galloped
over like a white horse heading back
to the stable. I took him home.
Made coffee while the kids stirred.
Watered tomatoes, cucumbers,
peppers, potatoes, asparagus, etc.,
gave the chickens a frozen zucchini
cut lengthwise to peck at, cleaned out
their water and said, There, there...
Did that big ole dog scare you? There,
there...I said. Checked for eggs.
Fixed the kids breakfast,
and somewhere in there decided
to open this computer and tell you
all about it, fingers knocking against
a digital space that belongs to no one,

acorns landing in irregular intervals
on the roof. I have a habit of putting
my needs aside. I have a habit
of breaking down eventually. I have
a problem with alcohol I seem
to have solved for the moment.
I try to be a good citizen, to express
patience with others, to shine lights
on daily happenings of negligible
import, to undress the cosmos
consensually. I wish I didn't hear
traffic in the distance. I wish
Regina and I could afford the farm
our minds have conjured. I say,
*Regina*, in a poem, and she always says
I should say, *my wife*, to make it
more universal. She's right, I know
she is, but I say her name anyway,
half expecting it to ask me to shut off
the lights and come back to bed. It doesn't.
The trash truck comes and goes,
and when I walk down to the curb

to fetch the cans I notice a red patch
of wild strawberries growing
near the street. I look closer.
I see them turning toward the sun.

# EVIDENCE

Fungus rehearses
its communion underground
as night rain coldly taps

a wooden cane, and the old
hound asleep by the door
twitches, dreaming the long

chase has ended with escape.
A peppering of lightning
followed by the arrival

of thunder. Neither stay.
Everything ephemeral
recedes back into waiting

while the sun raps
its mallets against the timpani
of horizon and fog

drags its bow evenly across
the rosin. Each woolen
sock slides over a heel.

The kettle clears
its throat. You take a long
knife across a lemon

as the kitchen window lets in
dawn. You stand there
quietly sipping, looking out.

# THEIRS AND THEIRS ALONE

The old Chrysler plant in Valley Park is gone
        in the way a body leaves this earth only once
and completely. For months, machines

        chewed and hauled it out as scrap,
and now, driving by on the highway,
        it looks flat as a wheat field after the harvest,

a solitary crow pulling his wagon of feathers
        in circles overhead. What became of the men
who still haunt the assembly line, which

        is only the early morning autumn fog
sloughing the Meramec river? What union is there
        for the displaced, the discarded, the bought out,

the pensionless men with mortgages
        on houses that seem a lot more temporal
as they wake and dress and slip outside

        for a smoke? It's cold, they think, colder
than they remember, and they strain their eyes
        to see an animal lurking along the tree line.

It glimmers before it's gone and the sun
          is late as usual and no matter what you think
about them they don't want your pity

          or sympathy or empathy or money.
They want the short drive to the highway
          in a vehicle they helped to assemble, to a job

that still exists, to the plant brought back,
          piece by piece from the scrapyards,
reassembled in fantastic celluloid rewind.

          And no matter what you think, they're not
suicidal when this doesn't happen.
          They don't want you imagining them

lining the brass rail at the Stratford Inn
          (which still sits directly across the highway
from the old plant), saying good riddance

          to a bucket of beer one slow, sad
sip at a time. And they don't want me either.
          Period. They don't want questions about

immortality that are only profound
        in the asking. They don't want angels
dancing on the head of a pin or riddles

        or games or magic tricks or miracles or fortune tellers
or palm readers deciphering the sum total
        of their life from a line on their hand

that seems a lot deeper now than it did
        twenty years ago. It doesn't matter to them
that my father worked summers at the plant

        to pay for college or that it was the worst job
he ever worked, in his words, in a life of shitty jobs.
        They only want to be left alone:

out of the news, out of poems, out of sight,
        out of the pain they wake to but don't call loss,
out of the empty field they drive by,

        the old plant still hidden in the fog,
out of the end they could see coming
        from the beginning, out of the days,

out of the nights, out of the stars shifting
            constellations, out of the epic pages of history,
which have no room for men who simply

            want to live without insult or injury,
out of the house and onto the back porch
            where they can smoke and enjoy the simple

pleasure of a body coming to life again
            like a machine, out of the smoke rising
from the exhaust of a pickup that no longer

            seems real—the plant where it was built is gone,
and the men who built it have dispersed
            with the morning fog. On the TV in the kitchen

they see a terrorist in Stockholm has blown himself
            in half on accident, a martyr of one,
and for the first time in their life they understand

            the anger of the discarded, how it builds
and builds until there's nowhere left for it to go,
            how their body holds them

and how they've grown to love it over time
        as deeply as they've loved anything
or anybody in their entire life because it is all

        that stands between them and the grave unknown,
and because men make promises they cannot
        keep. They think about the rain falling in Sweden

and remember too the first drops speckling
        their windshield as they sat in the parking lot
outside the plant one morning wondering if this

        was all there was to life, letting the coffee grow cold
in the cup-holder, until the sky finally opened up,
        and it started to pour—it felt as though

they were completely underwater,
        the white noise of downpour made everything
quiet and they didn't care if they were late or if

        they never worked another day in their life
or if the world just up and blinked out altogether.
        They knew you were out there soaking, waiting

for the rain to slow, till you could see them again
            sitting there like an instrument grown quiet
in its case. They knew how far you had come

            across time and space for this one moment of peace,
and how you wanted to take some of it
            for yourself. But if they had a revelation

inside that truck, it was theirs and theirs alone.
            The stars kept their order in the heavens behind the clouds,
and you got soaked. Soaked to the bone.

# AUTUMN

—after Apollinaire

My grandfather carries a canvas satchel, thumbs a ride
from the shoulder receding to gravel and ditch, receding
to a cropless pasture, which holds last year's broken tractor.

And over the carnival of passing traffic he shouts
and curses the luck of gods and men,
his voice whirring out the mechanics of failure.

To him, this season could be any, for they conspire.
Over the crest of the next hill taillights keep disappearing.

חֹשֶׁן

My only advice is not to go away,
Or, go away. Most

Of my decisions have been wrong.

—*Larry Levis, "In the City of Light"*

## WHERE WE ARE GOING

In this, the forty-fourth year of my life
on Earth, I look back on my heritage,
which is the crumbled red brick façade

of burned-out warehouses on the edge
of a river that is more American
than I can stand. The men in my family

grow quiet each Christmas when
salamini and cabbage, a peasant's dish,
goes round the table, and our old Torino

becomes a red wine that soaks up nothing.
It's easy to believe something sacred
has been lost. It has. It's easy

to lean against the headstone of a grave
that waits to be filled with your body
in a cemetery nobody visits more

than once and say that we are not where
we have been but where we are going.
Perhaps this too is a lie. My only birthright

is the Mississippi rising and falling
against a St. Louis that was built
with a brass note, which escaped the mouth

of a trumpet and traveled to New Orleans,
where the current slowed to a glass of ice
and bourbon and quickly disappeared.

# CARMINA BURANA

Strings warm rosin in the orchestra pit
as an usher catches my wife's earring
with his flashlight beam—his white gloves
another decadence in this scenic cantata.

My own music career ended at age ten when
I traded in my viola for a steel-cage match
between the "Macho Man" Randy Savage
and the Ultimate Warrior—a masculine

spectacle, testosterone at its most theatrical—
and the strings of that sold instrument changed
into a chain-link cage lowered from the ceiling,
changed into two men swollen with steroids,

costumed in spandex, glistening baby oil
for pay-per-view cameras and living rooms,
everyone unwrapping their microwave dinners
at the exact same moment.

Some twenty years later, in a plush seat
at Powell Symphony Hall, I'm not thinking
about the Goliards or the bawdy paradise
of the flesh, only the news of Macho Man's

death by heart attack and how I never
saw him break character—ever. Looking back,
I would've sold a million violas just to have known
what he was thinking inside that cage that night,

what my father was thinking inside that arena,
standing next to me, watching men his age
desperate to pin each other, the referee's palm
falling flat against the canvas. Was it catharsis?

If, *the play's the thing,* as Shakespeare said,
then what is the actor who loses his stage?
What is retirement to a body wasted and a heart
weakened by cycles of winstrol and anadrol?

And what does it mean to trade music
for instruments of the flesh,
for the pinup gladiators who never grow old,
who never die as dramatically as they lived?

I'm holding my wife's hand now as the baritone
clears his throat backstage and the audience
applauds the conductor's arrival,
"O Fortuna" poised on the tip of his baton.

The truth is I wouldn't change a thing.
I was no prodigy, and that stringed instrument
was nothing more than a wall standing
between a father and his son.

And when those giant men threw their bodies
at each other with reckless abandon,
didn't my father look down at me and say:
*Don't worry son, none of this is real.*

## ELEGY FOR THE MISSISSIPPI

It wasn't until '93, while I stood in the middle
of the shutdown interstate watching
the disemboweled Mississippi drag a farmhouse

across its breached levees,
that I understood how something as simple
and plainspoken as a river could empty the words

from its tongue and slink off
like a dog to die in the weeds.
My father stood next me, speechless, the same man

who taught me to manage a current with a paddle,
and when that lesson failed,
how to loose a canoe

from a snag—his wedding ring slipping
off his finger as he pried us free, sank golden
into the water, into the silt.

At eighteen I inherited a St. Louis
run dry of commerce, Powell Square gutted by its banks,
red brick and missing teeth,

scrub tangling its tarred roof, cobblestone shores
turned into parking lots
for steamboat casinos

and floating jazz bands—this
became my American dream: rattled warehouses,
train yards, titty bars and all-night discos,

Mississippi Nights and barstool booze poured down
my throat
from the neck of a tilted bottle—

fill that empty bottle
with gasoline, stuff a rag down its throat
until it's soaked
                              and ready to burn.

This is the body of the Mississippi,
gummed with soot and slicked with oil.
This is where my dream finally disappears.

This is an elegy not about loss
but about the losing:
it's about my father muscling a canoe loose

from roots, the tan line on his ring finger fading;
it's about bracing myself
to vomit and it's about the vomit itself

rushing between the grouted cobblestones
until it met what was left
of the Mississippi, dead as it was,

and the river took me in as one of its own.
                              *Big River,*
I was born too late,

never knew the men so ambitious
they thought they might tame you
although barges still swear to that ambition,

passing in their slow way south, uneager.
And only now do I understand
as I watch those vessels sag into your current

there can be no remorse among men
and the sludged water
they craft into lock and dam.

# CUSTER

Reader, you're not American and never were
really because America is just a word,
which is itself an Italian road leading back
to Rome, but travel long and hard enough
and you may bear witness to the path
of failed ambition from the once wannabe
president of these states along a road lined
with a charred national forest that bears
his name, and then you'll come to Busby,
reservation of the northern Cheyenne,
which dribbles out of Rosebud Creek and
flashes a blinking yellow stoplight swinging
inside a dust devil next to a giant teepee
constructed out of weathered shaker
shingle siding. Some version of inherited
guilt in you might flare up as you pump
gas in the pretense of present tense, but
that guilt really isn't yours either. Don't think
for one second you can untrouble
Big Horn County by tucking a day white
cumulus into a child's shirtfront pocket
and watch him rub it like his own little

lucky charm while pronghorn go on
tenderizing the indifferent high plains.
Redemption isn't a thing one offers oneself
with its multi-syllabic longing for, and
forgiveness isn't waiting in Rapid City
where descendants of the Sioux
blow ancestral music forth from
wood flutes for their children and
for anyone who'll listen. Listen friend,
you're safe here and chances are you're
a nice enough person, but that doesn't
make you a song without end. You
are the paved path from a meandering
stream to a wagon wheel swallowed
by sagebrush, and you will still have
to choose between a day at Crazy Horse
or Mount Rushmore, or say fuck it and
drive altogether through nowhere until
you finally get to Evans Plunge expecting
the hot springs there to be hot, but they're
not. The Sioux and Cheyenne who battled
over the springs just outside these black hills

could have told you that, but we don't ask
questions we don't want to know answers
to anymore. Try instead taking a mountain
of red shale and grinding it down to powder.
Mix it with one hundred quarts of horse
blood, and rub your eyes with it until
the roads disappear into foothills. Take
both hands and unroll that Pontiac Sunfire
from the field of switch grass and somehow
pry open the windows on all the clapboard
shacks and thistle-eaten double-wide
graveyards from there to Pray, Montana.
Maybe this is the closest to a crown we ever had.

## AFTER THE MISCARRIAGE

Nothing fixed
what couldn't fix,
and there were
no synonyms
for misscarriage,
no inherited
wisdom
for how to let go
of that which
existed, no way
to use the
names that
we'd discovered
like blackberries
hidden away
in the darker edges
of the forest.

Almost
nobody knew
that any of it
had happened,

and already bits
of dust were
settling onto
bookshelves.
There was
no space
in which
to grieve,
no context for us
to bury it in,
and so our grief
became a berry
rebounding
from last year's
unplucked bramble,
returning to
the same length
of thorn and
growing into
familiar form.
It's how
the invisible
becomes

visible again—
different
each time,
I guess,
but similar.

For a while,
she kept the list
of names
on her nightstand
before they
folded back
onto themselves
like prayers
or childhood—
proper nouns
breathing
like fireflies
between trees,
and our bodies'
insistent hunger
begged us forward
and we went.

## MORNING CIGAR ON THE EDGE OF A LAKE IN PENNSYLVANIA WITH BOETHIUS

Say, what kind of bird is that crying over my shoulder?
I'm smoking a cigar in the morning, which is not healthy,
but look, that fish just took something from the surface.
A water strider or derivation? Then a blank rippling out.
What am I searching for in all this mist over the water?
I cannot function correctly any longer as I have ceased
to be of efficient design, like any machinery, leaning
towards a new state of entropy. Take my eyes for example.
They are poor and strained—even now!—and make
bird watching impossible. I used to be late to my own
parties. Now I skip them altogether. Who would go?
I think, or is somebody working on the algorithm
for sweet magnolia other than bumble bees which hum
even though humming went out of style with the Tooth
Fairy? Why do we still lie to our children so fantastically?
I've grown up and left behind the commerce of pillow coins.
In my opinion, Wall Street seems too focused on getting it
right, that it forces jumpers off the ledge when they get it wrong
too often, or maybe I'm just mistaken in my understanding
of the macro-economic-global-infrastructure-gross-
archaic-domesticus-Frito-Banditos. I got lost just there.
I have no idea how the wealthy sleep. Well, I suppose.

I'm smoking a cigar at this moment and this one too.
Investing in a field guide or Wikipedia would give us all sorts
of interesting language right now, I mean, who doesn't like music?
That bird is still crying over my shoulder, so perhaps
I'm stuck in a loop. Since I cannot see the bird,
nor do I possess the will nor the binoculars to see said bird,
that bird may not be realer than the mist which
is not gone either. It keeps drifting in from the woods.
Maybe there's a mist machine pumping it down to the lake
from high up atop that hill over there. The wind is just right.
The wind has never been not right unless a person had hoped
to go another direction, in which case I'd have suggested
taking to the wing or lowering one's expectations. My dad said
low expectations make living possible. My therapist
said I need to live in reality and stop projecting.
My archangel made a noise so loud my head exploded.
Thinking for myself has been out the window ever
since, but I've adjusted accordingly and am smoking
my cigar again right now. Honest means you're
unhidden. If you want a doctor's help, uncover a wound.

# BUTTERBEAN

*My name can get them here the first time, but if you don't have good food, you can't keep them coming back.*

—Eric Esch, aka Butterbean (the semi-famous professional boxer from Jasper, Alabama discussing his new BBQ joint)

In her blurb for August Kleinzahler, Vendler says the poet
certainly gets *the maximum out of the minimum,*
and it takes a second for me to realize the serrated nature
of that praise. Perhaps that is the nature of all praise,
I think, as my daughter stretches her legs into a pair
of unicorn patterned leggings and sets off into the wild
neighborhood to go ride her bike and wander unchecked,
which seems like an art form that's been lost to her generation.

We have a big hill at the end of our street. She's been
sizing it up for weeks and that's where she's gravitating
with her long loops back and forth in front of our house,
and I suppose now is as good a time as any for me
to confess to you that I've never trusted Homer's wandering
Odysseus, because his journey seems a bit forced, doesn't it?
Look, these were seafaring people for the love of God.

War mongering, sharp witted, maritime men with long ships
and a wealth of expendable sailors. The answer is, Yes!
They knew enough to avoid having to navigate home
for hundreds of pages, and, thinking now, I suppose
I should admit that I'm no better, with me and my family
and our spur of the moment idea to raise chickens
on our first-ring suburban plot—it took a ten-year-old boy
down the street to tell me the chickens make a bunch
of noise when they lay eggs, and all I'm thinking about
now is the use of *lay* or *lie* and how I still avoid the verb
altogether because I've never been smart enough to master it.

What have you mastered? Do you think Vendler would just
shrug her shoulders and cut you an even break? Jesus Christ,
we're talking about *The New York Times* like it's just some rag!
But also, I should confess to you that a dear friend
and former colleague of mine asked me to write a poem—
not this poem, exactly—for her daughter who's graduating
from Washington University, which was why I sat down
with Kleinzahler in the first place—for inspiration—and
because I don't believe in the austerity of saying no
to an unlikely commission. What sense of misplaced

decorum about the realms from whence poems
and poets depart and return to would I be appeasing?

*The Aeneid* was nothing more than a graduation gift
for Rome, so yeah, ask yourself why Virgil didn't write
a poem for someone more appreciative than a benevolent
emperor who never not once had to draw his own
bath or skin his own grapes? Why do we feel the need
to escape our upbringing so much that we aspire
towards greater shores than the muddy rivers that birthed us?

It's no surprise I'm thinking about the boxer Butterbean,
for no other reason than he came to mind and this is still a poem
that I'm at the helm of, for what it's worth. The man weighed
in at over 400 pounds and had to go on a *butterbean diet*
to cut weight to box in the Alabama Toughman Contest.
Origin of the nickname and the oblong trajectory of his career.
Now he's back in Jasper serving lunch and dinner at his own
BBQ joint and he's happy and I don't know why this is so hard
for people to understand. I tell my children they should be

grateful more often than they are when they misbehave
in spite of all the reflexive gestures of parenting I offer up.
What would Vendler say of my children? Perhaps they too
are simply venturing out on their own fledgling sagas
of leaving and returning. It's too early to tell. Still, I can
stop writing long enough to watch my daughter on her bike
as she disappears down the street. The minutes pass, and
the last I saw she was aiming her wobbly bike toward the hill
I never once told her she could or could not ride down.

## SPINY ORBWEAVER

She's lingered a week now
with impressive ease upon
a latticework of anchor
lines that run from porch
railing to dogwood elbow
back to porch swing and post,
so when a slight wind
moves through, the whole
apparatus sways and dips,
just ever so, as the tree
limb it's anchored to also
sways and dips. There are birds
waking and chipmunks
darting across the flagstone,
and the leftover rain from
a hurricane has followed
the Mississippi River Valley
north and will be here
by noon. I look at the spider.
She looks at I know not what.
She survives the mild end
of this mild August hardwired

to a reservoir of silk and
dazzling exoskeleton. She lazes
upside down and waits
for a moth or mate to arrive,
and soon enough the onset
of cold will rub her away
from this earth like a spec
or smudge of dirt from my
glasses. Soon enough, yes,
but not yet. No, not yet.

# MARIZIBILL

—after Apollinaire

The Ozark lake where she grew is wrecked
with the pallor of winter and out-of-work
Johns, with slow boats, with houses pecked
clean of families. Trifles of smoke and sex
littered the bar where I once sifted ore

in bourbon neat. She was the dartboard
that locals took shots at, nailed, and became
nothing more than imagined air in this crude
place, a smear of brass rail moored to the bar's
lip, a dartboard's smooth and untouched frame.

## ART FAIR

I came to meander through open-air booths erected
in the name of self-taught metallurgical fiends
who curl lengths of iron into abstract lawn décor,

in the name of grade school art teachers
who scrawl feverish landscapes into the night,
in the name of potters who breathe and bellow fire

into backyard kilns, in the name of woodworkers
who turn burlwood into bowls for still-life prints.
I came here because there exist people with second lives

that last longer than the first, and because we all
eventually fall into the shapeless crowds who wander
these grassy lanes like ghosts who've fallen

into portraits tacked in museum galleries. If I fail
to bargain down a smear of moon oil on canvas, just watch
me move in on that bloodwood cutting board,

or that hand-twined chandelier, because there's a price
in my head that's incapable of change and all it takes
is a bit of small talk and to look someone in the eyes?

I once convinced a man at a roadside fireworks tent
to knock ten bucks off a 12-pack of Mississippi Gambler
mortar shells so I could paint the night with more color

than you can imagine, and he just sat back into his body
and his impossibly quiet lawn chair. Just sat back down
into a life defined by a carnival tent of powder and fuse.

Listen, I came here to feel a rougher art rush through
each one of my eye's billion vessels, because color
and form, and because far from the Louvres

of the world artists still find ways to fashion
grief into the arcades of other people's hearts.
Because somewhere near these tents meat smoke rises

from pork fat spit into embers, and because somewhere
there is a moveable stage upon which a bass player
slowly unlatches his case, and because soon enough

the lights of this art fair will begin to dim, and each
one of us will drift back to the silence of our homes
where we will each unearth from slumber the stud-finder,

level, hammer, and a single nail in order to hang
an image upon the dining room wall
where before there was nothing, until now.

# THE BLACK WHEELBARROW

Having owned the wheelbarrow long enough
to know one hundred percent of the time the tire
will be flat when I go to fetch it, I went with
the punctureless solid rubber option to serve
my hauling needs for the remaining life
of the wheelbarrow. I got it from Lowe's,
because I was told The Home Depot supports
the re-election of Trump to the tune of millions,
and after buying the tire a meme reminded me
to shop at Lowe's because the orange store supports
the orange president and the blue store supports,
well, not him. I felt the way lab mice must feel
when they reach the end of the maze
after a string of sleepless nights, but when
the feeling vanished it was gone and I set out
to change the tire—straight-jaw tongue-
and-groove channellock pliers was all the job
took. You ever smile and lie and say *fine*
when a friend asks how you're doing and then
they pry a bit more to see what's going on
inside? See, I found out that The Home Depot
retired its Trump supporting board chair Bernie

Marcus almost two decades ago, that the company
vocally doesn't support the orange president,
and here I was thinking I'd achieved some
version of moral equilibrium but I was wrong.
There was a letter on justice and open debate
that appeared in *Harper's Magazine* signed by like
one hundred and fifty writers who have that kind
of brand recognition writers like me appreciate,
but then Twitter found out, and boy was it pissed.
I've never heard war drums start up in earnest,
but I imagine that's what it must've sounded like
in the heads of the social media horde as they
considered link, meme or gif—life is all about
choices, isn't it (thank G-d nobody reads beyond
titles anymore! I think we can still be civil!)?
But yes, how many readers of poetry (show of hands)
own wheelbarrows? Or chickens for that matter?
I've got one black wheelbarrow and six chickens.
One chicken is a white leghorn: her name is Happy.
Remember Foghorn Leghorn? I do. Sweet Jesus
he was a big chicken and probably an outlet
for the creator's racist tendencies and simultaneous

contempt for the confederacy. I've been told
by those who've been born into strong accents
how important it is to lose the accent if you want
to succeed in academia. Gardening is okay work,
but I wonder if there's a limit on how many power
tools one can own and still be a reasonably
well-received professor? I'm sure I've exceeded
my limit—my six-hundred dollar DeWalt compound
miter saw makes me want to own a truck. I'm thinking
Toyota Tacoma, but I've got a good history
with Toyotas so I must say that I'm a bit biased.
I actually got the wheelbarrow tire for my wife
who was going to haul the rest of the firewood
from the front yard to the woodpile in back
next to the shed, but we talked late into the night
about the fucked up soul of our nation, of all nations,
how human history seems like one big contest
to see which form of torture is the cruelest—there
is nothing new under the sun—and go figure, today
we're suffering, depressed and generally blue.
I read some of Betts's book *Felon* before I started
this poem. I was reading his poem "Confession"

before I started this one (antecedent could be either
poem or confession), and I feel I've gone somewhere
different. I believe that's worth mentioning.
That we need not depart with an arrival in mind
as we sift our way through the language. But being
as I am a human and not just a collection of words
hustling to get in line when the reader flips the light
switch on the wall, I should confess I'm still grieving
the death of my mentor—a poet who worked to be
counted among the greats to hail from New Jersey.
I didn't remember the grief till this moment in the poem.
You see, he never wrote about a wheelbarrow
that I know of, but if he had, he'd have made it clear
that a wheelbarrow is just a vessel we're meant to fill
and guide and ultimately empty. It makes the work
a bit easier, and the load may seem a bit lighter,
but the work is still just work, waiting to be done.

# NEWTON'S CRADLE

Trains are not an expression
of benevolence: fixed and heavy
and always lurching through
like a caravan of wheeled
elephants atop the silk road
of post-industrial America.
Look at all that empty space,
the flat plains and high deserts
full of rabbits and the leafy
tendrils of interstate pilgrims
bound for their respective
Gracelands. Goodwill remains
a soft skill though, not
transportable, not a commodity
like butane or cyclohexane,
which both must be as useful
as they are combustible.
Of course they lope,
train cars like businessmen
and women and persons
counting down the days
till retirement with a black

sharpie, sniffing the black
tip before putting it away.
Another X. Another night
in the townless wonder
of neither here nor there.
There's a schedule trains
are always keeping ahead of
even if that's hard to imagine.
Humans are in there, too, still
at the engine's yellow helm.
If you live near the tracks
you could be like me and dig
up occasional railroad
spikes from the ground,
rusted and flecking
to crumbles—for the betterment
of what? At the crossing,
in this Oldsmobile of a poem,
the museum walls of graffiti
pass before our eyes—
little panicked etchings,
the medium of youth. They

pass before us like sonnets
of train yard cat and mouse
flashlight games in the darkest
corners of less valued parts
of cities. The yards of trains
are where the tracks breed
in twilight and wend into
and out of one another
with cosmic radiance.
Like a Russian ballet company.
In full disclosure, it's now
two thousand and twenty
and there's Amtrak Joe
from Scranton who seems
to posses some version
of childhood innocence
mixed with the anger of grief,
which is a combination
that seems like an old-timey
tonic meant to help one sleep,
only, not very soundly.
He should have retired,

all things considered,
but it's five days after
the election and we don't yet
have a president and our family
is plotting an escape
from this country should
our democracy collapse
like meringue. Regina
and I stay up late playing
scenarios and compare
strategies: pistol, holster,
passports, cash, emergency
packs (already in the cars)—
west or east or north,
depending on the prevailing
winds and the fallout.
Will Canada even let us in?
Will the coal still be driven
from its mountainy slumber
to be busted and loaded
into the cars to keep the lights
of houses flicking on? Will

produce be stacked
upon grocery displays,
apples like red pyramids
and cheeses sliced from
wheels which are not
the wheels of trains that roll
from one place to another
sharp enough to cut a human
in half if one gets tired and
lays a body down upon
the rails, closes one's eyes,
and hopes to be delivered
early like a package from
Amazon arriving on a Tuesday
because Bezos is the closest
thing we have to a baron.
Trains are always moving
at any moment of the day
or night and there is comfort
in that motion—think of
the device with those little
metallic balls swinging

and clacking atop the oak
of your therapist's desk.
The device has a name
just like you have a name.
Isn't that wonderful?
The energy locked
in the pendulum's
efficient swing—so little
goes to waste, so little
goes unnoticed—your
therapist, in this poem,
is actually my therapist,
and her voice draws
you further down into
yourself until you're
submerged—why are you
anxious? she asks, what
is this formidable ennui?

וֹרְחָס

I've lost the way.
O dream, come back for me.

—*Chase Twichell, "A Seduction"*

# FRAMEWORK

We'd found ourselves in Memphis, Cologne,
Boston, then Lyon. We discovered churches,
escarpments, hillsides burnt to stubble and
the ruins of local bars flattened to rubble
for the onset of strip malls and boutique hotels.
We watched as trauma entered like detox
sweats on the third night, how it twisted
into a metaphor for the orchards and vineyards
and barnyards left to rot thanks to the usual
vehicles of displacement that rolled in from
out of state with bags of cash and bad plates.
We scratched like hens for love. We wasted
our time and money in the supermarkets.
We convinced ourselves that we knew
the firmament from the face of the lake
because that was a lie we could live with.

But suddenly, the tone was all wrong. We
were mid-life roustabouts debuting in white
at the dilettante ball. The salesman was our
father knocking on suburban doors with
tight knuckles and wrecking balls for fists.

We looked around in terror and saw the walls
were white as the emptiness surrounding
a stanza, and then we collectively blinked.
What changed in us was more feeling
than fact, more fog than mist. We lit a candle
in the basilica and flipped our collar up
as we pushed open the heavy wooden doors
stepping out into a street full of pedestrians
and shop windows refracting sunlight. It was
morning again, and each step forward
brought the world that much more into focus.

# HOTEL

From my top floor room I see the Washington
Monument bathed in pre-thuderstorm light.
It looks alone out there. It looks as lonely
as I feel standing in this window shirtless
giving not one thought to some voyeur's
telescopic lens touching me. I miss my wife
and children. I think it's okay to admit this now
to you in this space where we are both alone
and not alone in that weird poetic way. Hello.
Let me put a shirt on real quick and invite you
into my hotel room to stand on the throttled
carpet and talk about negotiating intellectual
property language for industry contracts.
It's just something I do from time to time.
Like how I might say a stroke of lightning
behind that phallic monument seems relative
to one's perspective, not meaning to make things
entirely uncomfortable, but you know
the phallus as well as I do makes people shift
in their seats. Maybe we're all just vessels
of orange light glowing the way coals do
in a fireplace towards the end of a night, but

hotel rooms don't have fireplaces. My house does.
I must rely upon my belief in the existence
of worlds beyond this one, lives beyond this life
I'm still sorting through, time that expands
beyond the need for time to a universe where
clocks are set to night-blooming cactuses
or the twirls of octopuses. I think you desire
as much from existence as I do. Do you
think of it as a sponge you're wringing dry?
Maybe that's just me. Maybe I'm the storm,
and maybe you're the monument rising
like a microphone from an empty stage.

# ECCLESIASTES

This girl at my daughter's school said her family
lives in a mansion, and now my daughter says so, too,
as we cut through the rich side of town and
drive past homes with tennis courts and heated
stony grottos that waterfall into mosaic tiled pools—
inspired by the ones in Santorini no doubt—and statues
of angels that rise from the center of the pools and blast
trumpets, water tumbling down like a musical note
only the wealthy can hear. Her family must be blessed,
I say, even though I know the girl lives in Shrewsbury
where there are no mansions to speak of, only bad debt
and potholes and troubled parishes and racism, and yet,
our house, which is not in Shrewsbury, must seem
tinier each day to my daughter. She's not old enough yet
to be embarrassed by the claw foot tub and moldy vanity
and giant hunk of underlayment and linoleum I ripped
out from the bathroom, set on the porch, because of mold,
smelled it like another emergency loan from the credit
union. Thank God we had a deep enough porch to store
the junk while we figured out how to finance the job,
me providing the labor and it's a wonder I'm still not

drinking. I'm saying that the bathroom has decorated
our front porch since February and it's spring now,
and Cora's getting older by the minute and must see
porches that aren't warped and leaning and weeping
the contents of the house. Listen, I'm trying to tell you
that I'm writing this poem and contemplating a tub
in front of me that's turned on its side like one of those
sad whales washed up on a beach with fifty pounds
of plastic in their belly. I'm trying to say that I wear
a sports jacket to work because I've worn through
the elbows on my shirts—people at work think I'm
putting on airs, but I'm actually just cheap and desperate
for something in my life not to wear out. The jacket
was my father's and each time I slide it on I feel him,
but how the fuck did we end up talking about me? Let's
get back to the mansion my house is not and the daughter
growing taller and wiser by the second and the truck
I'll need to borrow to get that tub off my porch
and the bathroom in disrepair while the crocuses
have come and gone and now the daffodils and
soon enough the naked ladies and mulberries
and blackberries and when I was young there was

a moment when I thought money was the salve
one spreads on the wound of poverty and so my
friend and I drove up to a mansion we admired
in the middle of the day and knocked on the door
to ask the owner what they did for a living. Nobody
answered—middle of the day, the two of us skipping
school to get high and trespass. Maybe there's
a lesson I'm missing that's buried somewhere
in these words and I should probably just try
and remember how to pray or go read the Bible.
But a freight train is cutting through this two-sided
town and I can feel the porch vibrating underfoot
and the train's so loud I'd be foolish not to hear it.

# AIR SHOW

Just like any other car in the Home Depot lot,
this lime green Lamborghini Aventador finds

a spot under a porcelain striped, sky-blue sky
on a 60 degree day in May in a valley

that sank under the Mississippi in '93
only to rise again into this outlet-mall

renaissance where we have all come
with coolers and lawn chairs and children,

here to this valley where I once held my nose
until the water slowed back into its banks.

But now *is* today, and a trickster bi-plane rallies
smoke trails until it seems all I've forgotten

has been forgiven. My children ogle warplanes.
My children lack context. Their bewildered

eyes glance upwards at the alien mothership
known as the B-2 Stealth Bomber the same way

the cavalry of World War I looked up
at the whole sky atwitter with dogfights as the ground

shifted beneath hooves. Here lies a floodplain
that no longer floods. There whomps

a Chinook with two sets of blades,
and a Harrier Jump Jet pogos up and down

the runway like a circus elephant with wings
of steel, the whole show playing out like lost

b-roll footage from *Top Gun*, a film that was
nothing more than Tom Cruise's career

sliding one arm into an absurd leather jacket.
Patton, Napoleon, Alexander the Great,

even Achilles himself. When cast under
the dimmest light, don't they all just shrink back

into a failed treatise on free will? How is any age
greater than the hero it forges from iron

then scratches down into song or celluloid, and how
can our existence be proof of anything more

than the success of military parades of the past—a past
where parade goers squealed through flesh and

bone at the uniformed ranks trudging epaulettes
and tanks through commercial districts?

My children are squealing as loud as any.
My children are the relevance we bequeath.

My children are basking like lizards
under the swirl of turbine-induced jetwash,

and tonight they will fall asleep hard—I mean
they will pass the fuck out—sunburned, ears

still ringing—and when I click off the lamps and kiss
each forehead, I'll smell the jet fuel in their hair.

# EM DASH

Daydream Johnny's switchblade starting shit,
      the Aaron Burr of punctuation—you enter

every scene like Penelope's snubnosed suitors
      with throats slit and bleeding out into ending,

into interruption, parenthetical and beginning
      like an attention deficit problem-child, like ice

on hot coals raining back down as hailstones
      inside each thunderclap, monstrous storm,

leviathan of the underground tunnels, concrete
      storm sewer bursting forth an unswimmable

current against the boulder-smooth creek bed:
      the crawfish antennae, the fisherman's cast

from the lonely pier and of course the pier itself
      thrusting another argument into the Pacific.

Billy club, butcher knife, lead pipe, lipstick, flatline.
      Wild Thing strutting out from centerfield and the high

hard one breaking the strike zone's flimsy walls.
      Riptide, roller coaster jumping the tracks, mainline

delivery of juice and the lineman swaying down
      from a helicopter tether to a tripped transformer

with a song in his electric heart, grounded with rubber.
      You're singing Alpha's answer to Omega, Zeus's

lightning bolt to Hera's hand going up his tunic,
      and you're the steady playing drunk with a pool

cue in the pool hall cracking white cue balls open
        into rainbows. Cigarette on the doorman's lip,

unlit then lit. Movement without just cause,
        skipped heartbeat in the syntax. There's nothing

holding you back from the edge of the cliff
        from which you leap like dynamite and dive.

# ANIMAL MANIMAL

Phylum, phlegm, sperm and faces.
Fingernails, dovetails, askance.
Toenails, guard rails, entrails and flails.

Tyrants, tempers, tankers, toppers,
and tone-deaf singers alike.
Bury me and blitzkrieg and miscreant

and mead. Estrogen, endorphin,
mescaline, and magic. Happy hour,
scimitar, terrorize, and rage. Mister

and master. Blister and bastard.
Cages and orgasms and splinters.
Underwear, testicle hair, tire wear,

death stare. Rubber and clubber
and stutter and shudder. Zipper
and stripper and pisser and skipper.

Dung and sprung and sty. Wimple,
yokel, whimper, waver, dimple,
scamper, and trot. Fingers and phalanx

and oxen and robot. Marker and maker
and market and lot. Salt, sugar, spices,
and knives. Camper, saunter,

scamper, and stauncher. Loons
and logic and messy meconium.
Animal, manimal, scandal,

scramble, tongue ring, nugget,
and yacht. Whisper and wattle.
Tumble and topple. Pokers, strokers,

stokers, smokers, and soakers.
Genders and spenders and blenders on high.
Timely, slimy, icy, and spicy.

Asshole and foxhole.
Flaxseed and half breed.
Steam with a full scream ahead.

# THOREAU AT THE TRAILHEAD

I'm apex, bitches. I kick open
the door to my feral country
disparaged by snow
and burn the moon's long tongue
down switchbacks gorged
and strafed by bootcrush
to the river I canoe open
like a knifing of willow flesh.
I fashion a sway bridge
from bear sinew and heart strings
and cross wherever I please.
I cast a glisten and a bramble
and a canopy of coyotes
riffing a full-throated note
deep into the milky Milky Way.
To survive is mean, and I mean
to survive—if need be for weeks
on the fat of others and loose
berries and tubers I dig up
using my teeth like a shovel.
I make myself scarce and lonely.
I lilt like murdered sunlight.
I cache myself under a mountain
for when wild goes out of style.

## IF WE ARE HUMAN THEN LET US BE FOOLS

If my father had told me the secret
I'd pass it on now. Instead,

I'm just another abandoned zinc mine
in the middle of the country,

gladiolas on my wife's Sunday dress,
liver spot on the left wrist

of the dead bartender who baptized me
for nearly ten years. I was devout.

My father told me not to hoot with owls.
My father told me to soar with eagles.

My father told me that dedication and spite
were tributaries emptying into the same river.

My father told me that love was just an axe
that can't chop wood for shit.

Because you've failed to notice the orchards
dropping their bayonets each autumn,

you've come here for advice.
If we are human then let us be fools.

Let us keep turning to each other like children
pausing for answers to questions that always begin

and end with why. When winter comes, you'll know
it's your wife's birthday. When spring shows up,

buy it a drink. Spend the summer watching
a field of wheat fill its golden lungs with soil.

He stares out from a hotel
towering some strange city

and thinks of his wife
and children. He follows

the smokestacks littering
the industrious part of town

all the way up until they hit
clouds and begin to dream.

He recalls what his father
told him and feels the metal

in his chest grow brittle.
He sinks back into starched

linens and disappears
each night, just like that.

# I HAD THE COURAGE...

—after Apollinaire

but sold it for a beam of sunlight knifing
a hillside church in two.
It was like splitting an orange
to discover a gold coin
that a woman once choked on
while singing an ode to immortality.
Now, I can't recall much of my childhood
or the ghosts I emptied
from the Mississippi into that body
of saltwater waiting at its mouth.
I have sold off so much, gotten back
so little in return.

# HILLS

—after Apollinaire

When I stared too long into these Missouri hills,
they curled like slings around broken limbs,
and out came creepers edging the tree line, men with maps,
ancestral black earth, raw childless wind, water.
None of these things were mine. I gave them back

to a minister named Perry, so he might deliver them
from his Sunday pulpit, so he might
find within his open Bible an angel's wing
that holds a place, that holds a passage
from this Earth to the next, and he would keep it

for himself. That minister was and will forever
be a fool. He never did represent me
or my country which I gave back
and found waiting under the same
bridge I crept out from. When I was young,

our cherry tree squirmed its roots towards
China and brought the truly exotic
women within reach. Summer. Noon. I would
fall asleep under the canopy and dream of them.
I imagined their lips were already songs.

Women like that lit fires in the belly
of my father's Buick when it wouldn't
turn over. I watched him lug it from the garage,
beat the hood with a sledge and call it a lousy
American tramp. My father spelled disasters.

You could find him everywhere.
He was like these hills. He towered over
engines that misfired or didn't fire at all.
He knew the mechanics of anger
and frustration because his life

was complete and adorned with roadways
that led him to upper management.
I found it nonsensical, chose instead to let
a few musicians show me the true meaning
of a fifth of bourbon and a barstool

too far from any rocky coast to conjure
an ocean, this river had to suffice.
Stack-O-Lee shot Billy Lyons next to it.
Down near Morgan Street. He didn't shoot him
over a Stetson or cards. It was politics.

And then I became a man and acted like one.
I followed his trail to the city to find or buy love
somewhere in the music that boomed
from the stacks of steamboats
broken on the Mississippi's filthy shore.

I crossed over one night and came back
married to my own desires, which meant
I'd found the strip clubs and drank all night.
Someone called out the river's depth
as I passed over, and it began to rain.

The city tucked itself under its wing.
A barge dredged for constellations
in the water, and the youthful deities
of wine and dance got covered in it,
plastered in river sludge from head to foot.

I got into my car and turned away
from the sunrise toward the hills and ruins
of a speakeasy. Nothing left but a stone chimney.
Castlewood, Missouri. Al Capone sought refuge
when he was this way, heading for those

always distant hills, and soon the time came
when even I had to pull over and shake
the glitter of stripper from my jacket.
I felt like a big Italian woman. My great great
grandmother beating Sienna from her rugs

till its dust swelled in her lungs and she tasted
all the misfortune and suffering to come.
Even my death hovered in her strong arm
before it swooped and landed another blow.
Her veins, which were bluer than any river,

became a river worth living next to. That woman
never felt useless or outmoded a day in her life.
One morning, I went to grab the paper and minister Perry
was waiting outside chanting snakes. He lured me
to a fishing boat and set me into the river.

*This is God's river*, he said. *Your heritage is
as holy and wet as the noses of catfish under
this skiff.* I lowered my hat brim and watched two
squirrels scramble loose from oak branch
to maple and back for almost an hour,

one of them caught up in the rush of wanting
to be on top of the other. I busted the sun
peeking and smelled honeysuckle drifting
from the ether. It reminded me of those Chinese
women under the cherry tree singing

on the other side of the earth, in silk,
in clouds of red silk, and that's when I knew
I loved my father but could never replicate
his body. His back was as tall as a hill
rising to meet a red-tailed hawk

for breakfast. I felt his hands touch
my shoulders as gently as he touched
anything in his entire life, and although I cannot
understand the certitude of cosmologies,
I know that I was born late and frail.

My star hovered over the water at night
then sank under its unbearable weight.
I waved goodbye to the ghosts
of my childhood and married a woman
who was better than jasmine on my tongue.

She took me to a peasant's Paris to float
on the Seine, which was not my river,
which was not my cathedral or carnival feast.
There is no Mediterranean I can't absolve
with a garland of soot, thorn and backwater.

The church bells said goodbye and waved
the way an old man once shook out his hanky
to wipe the tears from the cheek of his bride,
my mother, her mother and every mother
who has borne a body of water that went

nowhere and stank brighter than the halos
of angels. My wife Regina came to understand.
She is the single sweetness I have tasted
and not turned bitter from, the tasting, fell
as a meteorite onto the string of the guitar

a Creole man with four fingers played.
His eyes were closed. He didn't know I was there.
He didn't know his harmonies sizzled in dry grass,
but he halted just the same and sipped an oyster
clean from its shell down to the gullet.

Later, a six-foot snake slipped into the graveyard
at my grandfather's funeral, climbed a tree, wound
its body around a branch and ate robin eggs
out of the nest, one at a time. It might have been
that guitar player. The eggs probably tasted

of freshwater oysters, and Perry's church choir
sang about a shopkeeper who never dies,
who only counts his stock and dusts
his shelves and waits patiently for the time
of burning grace to descend.

Their music scattered like seed. I listened
to the distant barge traffic curdle and knew
I could never leave home, even if I wanted to.
Regina and I watched that minister
bury my grandfather at our feet

in a pit on a hill with a black snake run up
the tree like the flag of this country.
He sermonized an afterlife without peril.
Afterwards, we walked a mile through blight
and found a hawk on a dumpster behind the Chinese

restaurant. It was still morning, but we could smell
last night's braised pork hanging from its beak.
To him, we were no bother.
His head dipped in and out of plastic bags
like a torch that can't be extinguished.

We settled into a cantina booth a few blocks
up the road. The footsteps of the waitress
startled me, and I felt I was being overdramatic.
Like how my father waited years for the mechanic's
whiskered prognosis: timing belt, thermostat

housing, sway bar, junkyard. The dead
abdicate these small privileges and disintegrate.
The gastronomy of hills takes over.
I ordered what passed for huevos rancheros
and went to the bathroom.

Pissing on that blue urinal cake felt nothing like Greece.
I never was a supplicant to Achilles.
My education was public.
The Mississippi creased the back of my country
like the spine of an open book titled *patriotism*.

I never fought pigeons for scraps to call breakfast,
never plucked the whites out of a man's eyes
in new issue boots. I daydreamed women
underneath a cherry tree, traversed
the glory of blue afternoon skies,

was tricked by a minister at the river,
waded into the current to be baptized.
There, knee deep in bilge, all my shortcomings
were forgiven, my doom made certain.
Nothing miraculous can be forestalled.

My father became the glorious red-tailed hawk
on the edge of a rancid dumpster,
the twentieth century.
Still, he square danced with my mother
every Saturday when someone booked

a caller, drifted from the dance floor
into an orchard and conceived a family
on a bed of constellations, the streaming hair
of apple trees, while all those men and women
who danced simply faded from the planet.

Funny. Our kitchen table had a pine veneer.
My father polyurethaned three extra coats.
It was like staring at a felled tree in a shallow
bend in the river every time
we sat down to pray.

All of this I'm remembering now, at a desk,
peeling an orange,
as the universe gets its virginity back
to lose again during the next meteor shower.
We may be reborn like this, although

most of us end up mounted to the wall
in a museum like a dull axe, as forgotten
and worthless as a coin buried in a hillside,
our bodies cursed or filled with baptismal light.
Only invisible things are worth weeping for.

When I was young I thought words like majesty
had a purpose and were not just decorations
for the divinely inbred, but I have been wrong
about many things. I held my wife by the tail end
in the elevator going up to our honeymoon suite,

and she had a current stronger than any Mississippi.
The clerk at the desk brought us ice in the morning.
A few years later we lost a week in a Parisian hostel.
It was abstract. The lost time boiled off as vapor.
Light streamed around her, changed her. Not holy.

The river wasn't holy. Nobody I knew would've dared
to eat a fish out of it. Not my father
until he became a hawk and gleamed,
and I don't know much about Apollinaire
other than how I imagine him, looking into the Seine

and thinking about the things that remain, weeping
for the things that disappear. I was dramatic
about my country once and tried to give it back
to some minister with his angel feather
tucked in a Bible that would get him to heaven,

and the Creole guitar player I listened to
at an oyster bar the night I met my wife became
a snake in a cemetery tree eating robin eggs,
became an omen or the flag of my country
or both.

I'm tired of retelling the story of the cosmos
one hill, one river, one great great
Italian grandmother at a time. I laugh,
and a sunset overtakes me, closes me down.
The natural world is full of this arrogance,

therefore I'm full of arrogance
with my minor secrets,
my small history rotting me from the inside out,
my sun stalled over the Missouri hills where
my father's Buick has finally rolled to a stop.

# NOTES

Section breaks are the original Hebrew from Psalm 18:11 (יָ֫שֶׁת "He made" וְחֹ֥שֶׁךְ "darkness" וְרִתְסֹ "his secret place") with KJV translation here. The section art was created by my brother Josh Mossotti who took the section titles for inspiration.

The opening line of "Du Jour" takes inspiration from a Banksy mural on Melrose Avenue in Los Angeles, California from 2006 (*I am out of bed and dressed—what more do you want?*).

"Theirs and Theirs Alone" mentions the suicide bomber Taimur Abdulwahab al-Abdaly who tried to set off a car bomb packed with gas canisters in a busy shopping street in Stockholm. The car caught fire and the bomber fled the scene before blowing himself up 300 yards away 15 minutes later, injuring two bystanders. The Chrysler factory it eulogizes was actually in Fenton, not Valley Park.

"Carmina Burana" is based on an actual story. I gave up playing viola in fourth or fifth grade. My father sold back the instrument and bought tickets to Wrestlemania at the St. Louis Arena (the arena has since been demolished) with money he got from the sale.

In "Elegy for the Mississippi" the phrase "Big River" harkens back to the Anishinaabe (Ojibwe or Algonquin) name for the river, "Misi-ziibi," which means "Great River" or "Big River." It also mentions Mississippi Nights, a concert venue, which is no more.

"Morning Cigar on the Edge of a Lake in Pennsylvania with Boethius" was written about (and at the edge of) Lake Lacawac, a 52 acre glacial lake preserved in almost pristine condition that was declared a National Natural Landmark by the U.S. Department of the Interior in 1966. The final line of the poem borrows from Boethius from *The Consolation of Philosophy*, Book I: "If you want the doctor's help, you must reveal the wound."

"Art Fair" is based on the annual summer art fair held in Webster Groves, Missouri on the first full weekend of June.

"The Black Wheelbarrow" references "A Letter on Justice and Open Debate" that was an open letter with 153 signatories originally published on July 7, 2020 in *Harper's Magazine*. The poem also references the book *Felon* by Reginald Dwayne Betts.

"Hills" owes a debt to the Dudley Fitts translation of Apollinaire's poem ("Les Collines").

Dedications: "Wherefrom Comes This Country Goes" is dedicated to the memory of Philip Levine; "Apocryphal Genesis" is dedicated to my mentor and guide Rodney Jones; "Contemplation of a Live Oak in San Antonio" is dedicated to Naomi Shihab Nye and was written about a specific tree in the backyard of Dan Hager and Angela Brazeal Hager; "Book(s) of the Dead" is dedicated to the memory of Kenneth Harrison; "Du Jour" and "Universal" are dedicated to my wife Regina; "Theirs and Theirs Alone" is dedicated to Barney Wilcox; "After the Miscarriage" is dedicated to the one we lost; "Morning Cigar on the Edge of a Lake in Pennsylvania with Boethius" is dedicated to my fellow angels Kerry James Evans and James Kimbrell; "Butterbean" is dedicated to Jenny Kiesel and her daughter Rebecca (commissioned as a graduation present); "The Black Wheelbarrow" is dedicated to the memory of my mentor and one of New Jersey's great poets, David Clewell; "Newton's Cradle" is dedicated to my therapist Jessica Davidson; "Air Show" is dedicated to Tom Cruise.

The cover art (front and back) was conceived of and created for this book by my brother Josh Mossotti. The labyrinth design on back cover (and preceding the Notes section) is a depiction of one that occupied the Cathédrale Saint-Etienne de Sens floor (the first gothic cathedral) from entry to nave until the stone floor was replaced in the 1760s.

# ACKNOWLEDGMENTS

A special thanks to the following publications where some of these poems appeared (some in slightly different versions):

*Arts & Letters:* "After the Miscarriage" & "Book(s) of the Dead"
*Asheville Poetry Review:* "Carmina Burana"
*Big Muddy:* "Elegy for the Mississippi"
*Catamaran:* "Evidence"
*Copper Nickel:* "Marizibill"
*EPOCH:* "Wherefrom Comes this Country Goes"
*Florida Review (Aquifer):* "Art Fair"
*Iron Horse Literary Review:* "Air Show"
*Italian Americana:* "Where We Are Going"
*Manchester Review:* "Hills"
*Moon City Review:* "Framework"
*New American Writing:* "Thoreau at the Trailhead" & "Animal Manimal"
*Poet Lore:* "I had the courage…"
*Potomac Review:* "Custer"
*Valparaiso Poetry Review:* "Autumn"
*Water ~Stone Review:* "If we are human then let us be fools"
*Western Humanities Review:* "Theirs and Theirs Alone"

"Carmina Burana" was a finalist for the William Matthews Poetry Prize and was nominated for a Puschart Prize. "Elegy for the Mississippi" was included in *Down the Dark River*, an anthology of Mississippi poems published by Louisiana Literature Press. Many of the poems from this book were part of the chapbooks *My Life as an Island* (Moon City Press) and/or *The Mechanics of Failure* (Poets at Work Press). Some poems in this book first appeared in *Racecar Jesus*, published in the UK (Eyewear, 2023).

Poems in this book have benefited from support from fellowships, grants, and residencies from the Regional Arts Commission, the Sustainable Arts Foundation, the Artist Residency at Lacawac Sanctuary, and the Living Earth Collaborative at Washington University,

There are literally hundreds of people who've touched my life and made it worthwhile. People who shaped me, knowingly or not, and by extension these poems: please know that I love you and am grateful and look forward to seeing you and hearing from you again.

Gratitude to: to my first readers Kerry James Evans, James Kimbrell, and Regina Mossotti; to Naomi Shihab Nye, Adrian Matejka, James Crews, Erin Quick, Stefene Russell, Katy Balma, and the Tick Tock Poets for their correspondence, guidance and friendship; to my mentors Rodney Jones, David Clewell (in memory), Allison Joseph, Jon Tribble (in memory), and Judy Jordan; to my fellow Salukis Mark Brewin, Hannah New, Amie Whittemore, and so many others; to Timothy Liu (for your vision, friendship and editorial eye), Sarah Wetzel, Rebecca Lauren, Jennifer Fiore, Tyler Noyes, Henry Israeli, and all the good folks at Saturnalia Books; to my parents, brothers, sisters, in-laws and extended family who've helped shape me behind the scenes; to my brother Josh for his collaborative workshops and creative symbiosis; to my wife Regina, daughter Cora and son James for their enduring love and patience—you mean everything to me.

*Author photo: Regina Mossotti*

TRAVIS MOSSOTTI's previous collections are *About the Dead, Field Study, Narcissus Americana,* and *Racecar Jesus.* He's been the recipient of the Miller Williams Poetry Prize, the May Swenson Book Award, the Christopher Smart – Joan Alice Poetry Prize, the Alma Book Award, and others. He is currently the Program Coordinator for Poetry in the Woods and serves as a Biodiversity Fellow in the Living Earth Collaborative at Washington University. Mossotti lives and works in St. Louis.